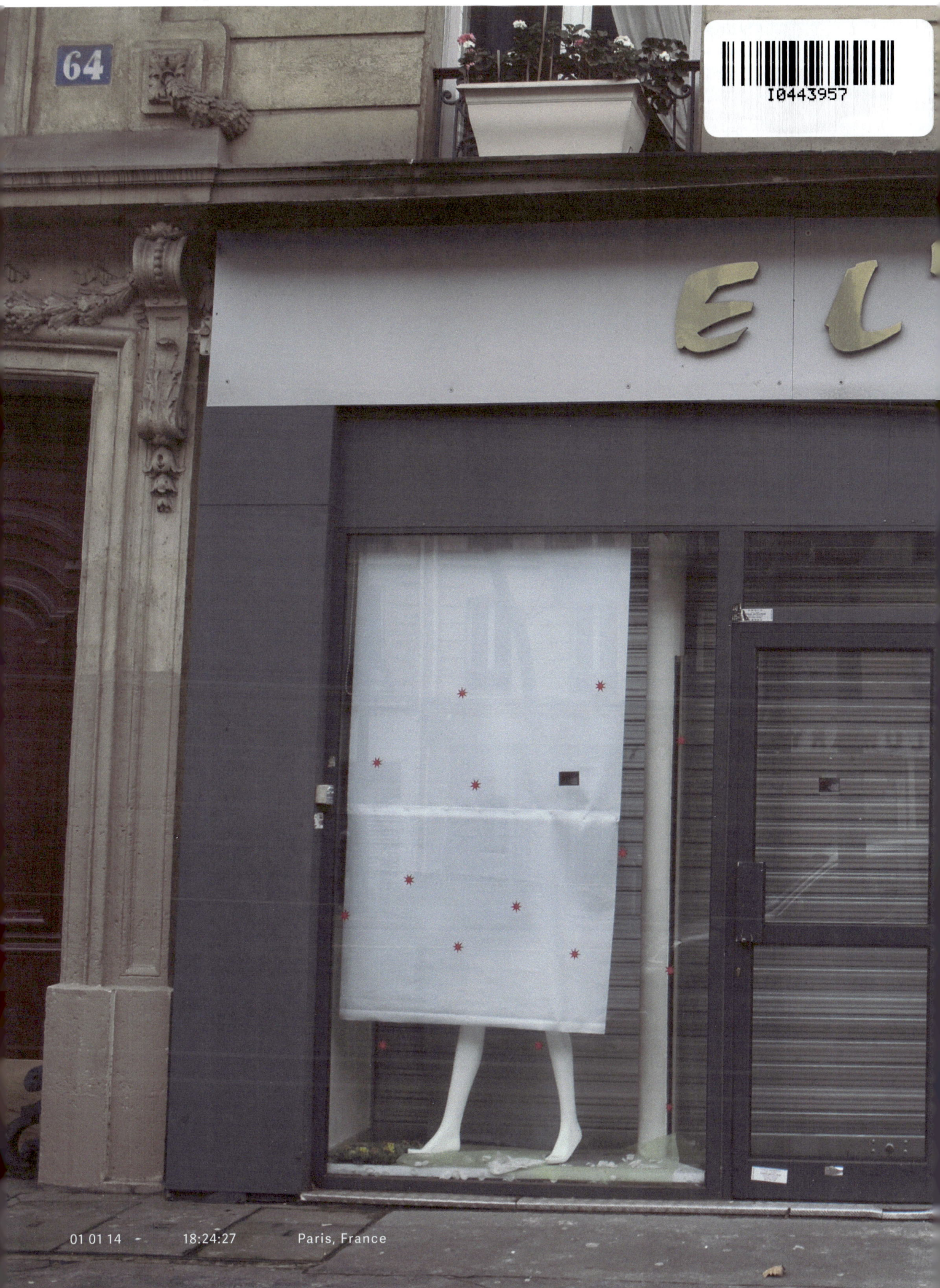

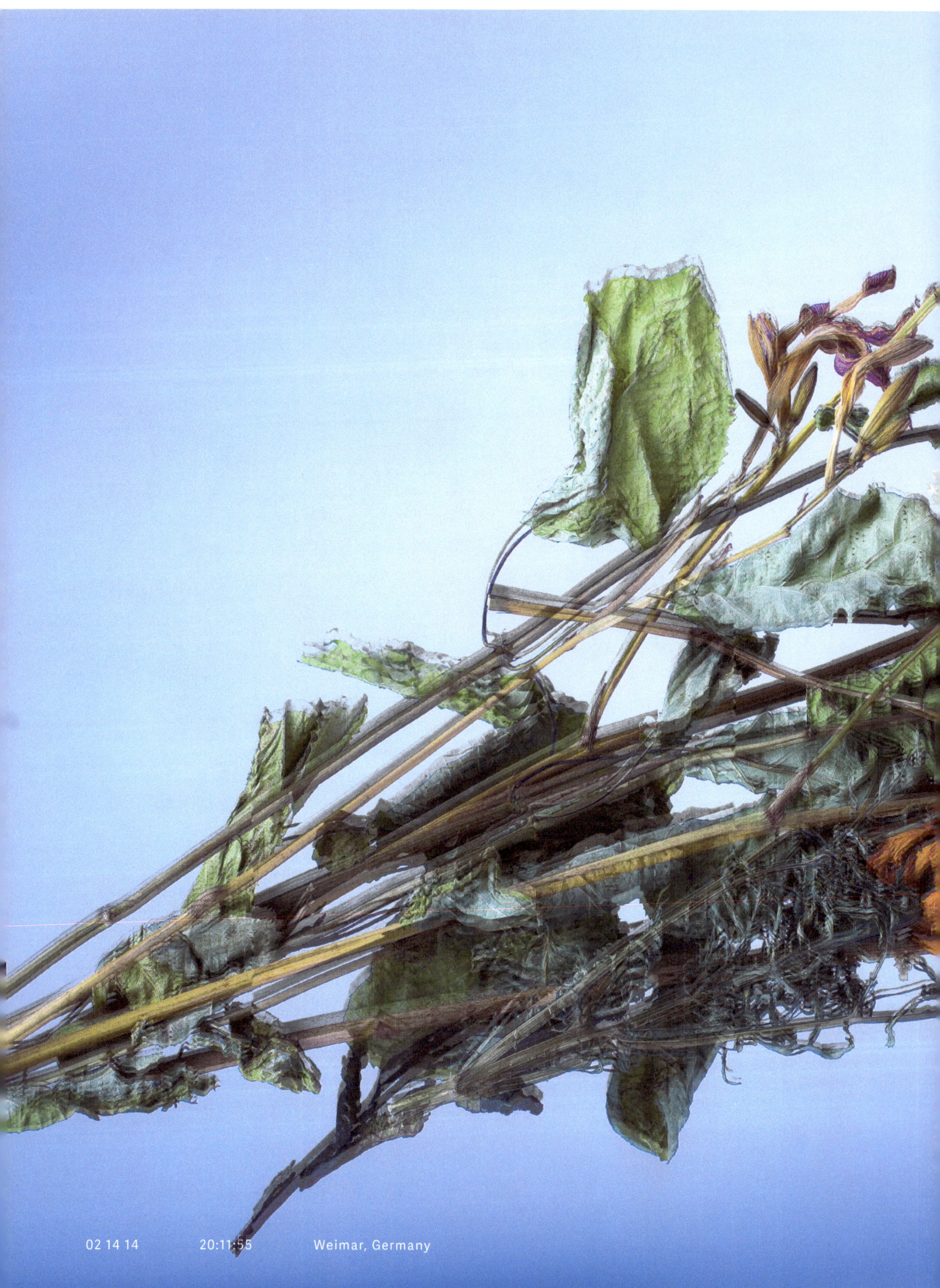
02 14 14 20:11:55 Weimar, Germany

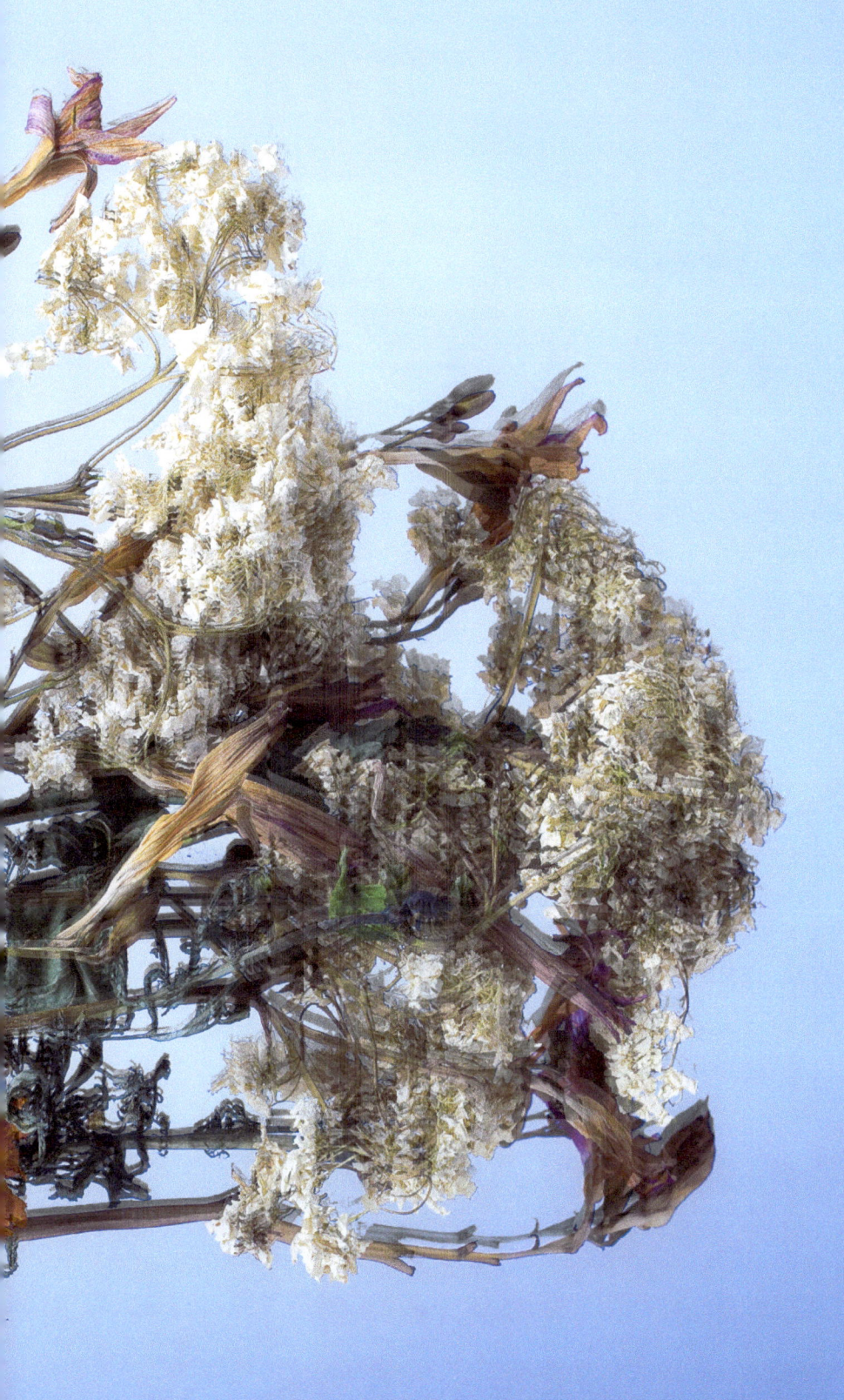

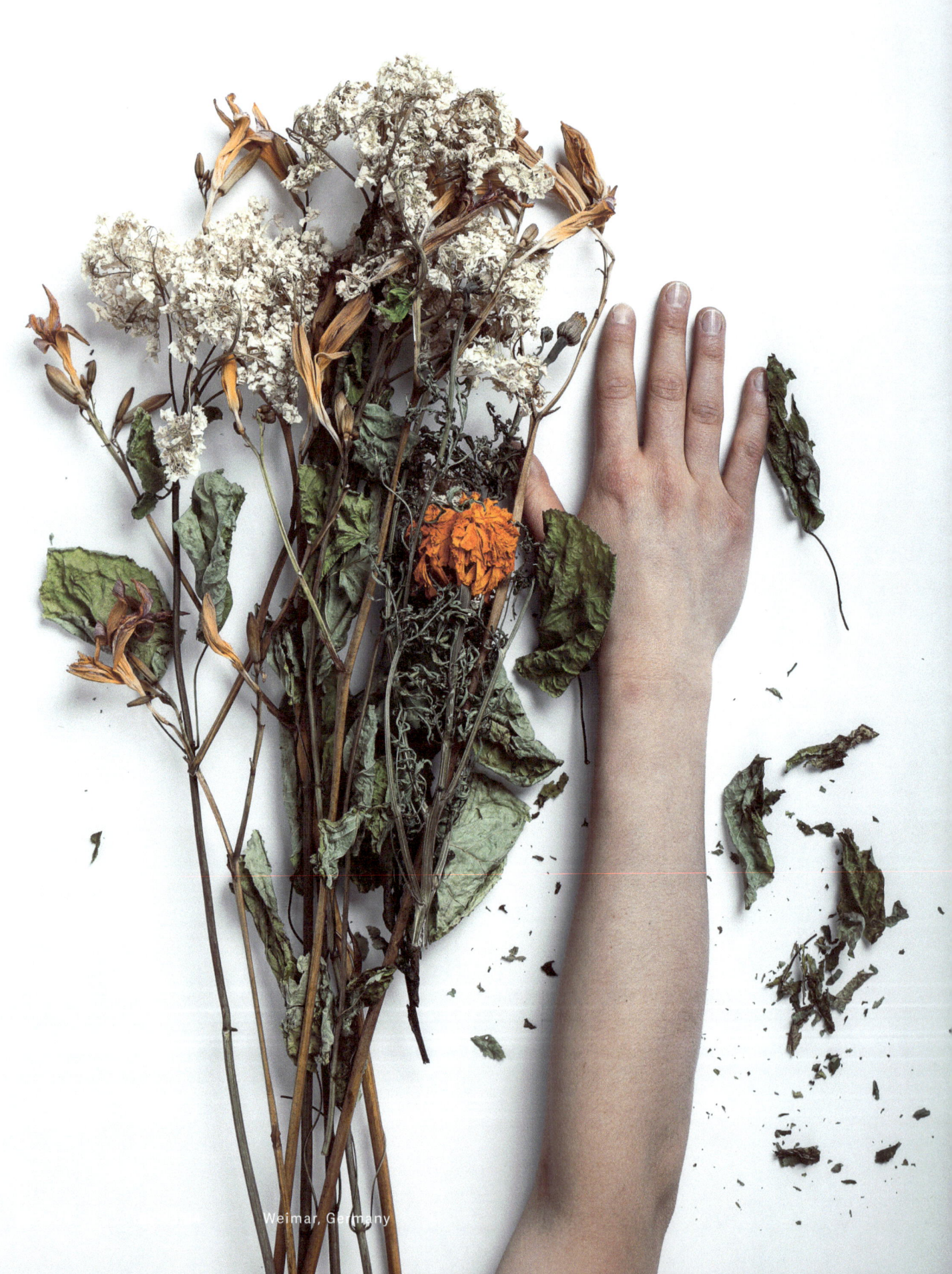

Weimar, Germany

	Date	Time	Location
1	01 01 14	18:24:27	Paris, France
2	02 14 14	20:11:55	Weimar, Germany
3	02 14 14	20:43:04	Weimar, Germany
4	02 22 14	14:58:21	Weimar, Germany
5	02 22 14	14:59:24	Weimar, Germany
6	03 07 14	17:46:19	Weimar, Germany
7	03 07 14	17:56:06	Weimar, Germany
8	04 26 14	15:54:27	Berlin, Germany
9	04 26 14	20:52:13	Berlin, Germany
10	05 27 14	21:12:38	Weimar, Germany
11	06 10 14	20:46:14	Weimar, Germany
12	06 10 14	21:49:09	Weimar, Germany
13	06 23 14	22:17:19	Weimar, Germany
14	07 09 14	20:38:03	Weimar, Germany
15	07 09 14	20:41:34	Weimar, Germany
16	07 13 14	17:38:21	Weimar, Germany
17	07 13 14	17:39:31	Weimar, Germany
18	11 09 14	21:11:27	Weimar, Germany
19	12 01 14	21:50:54	Weimar, Germany
20	12 01 14	21:55:11	Weimar, Germany

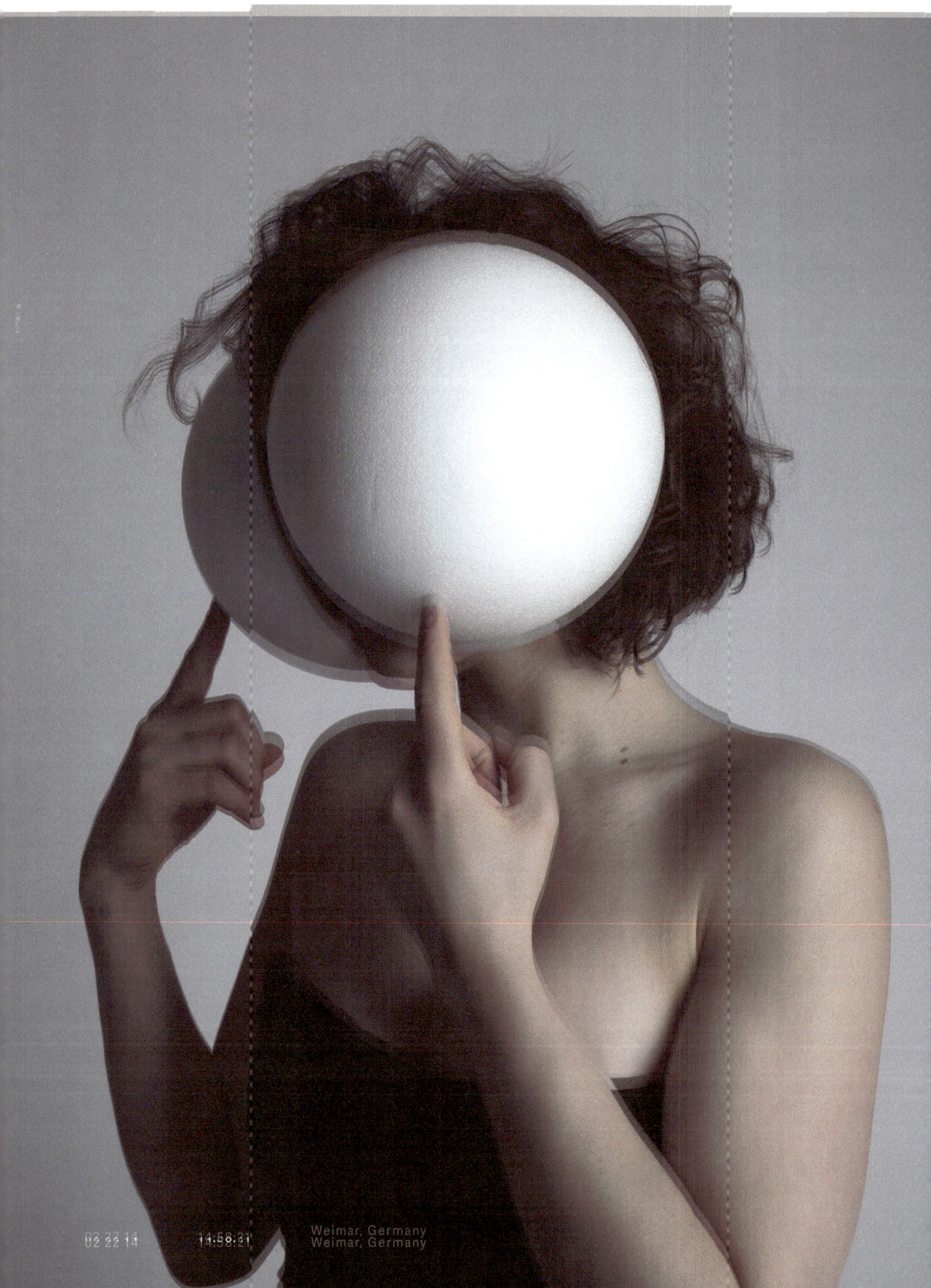

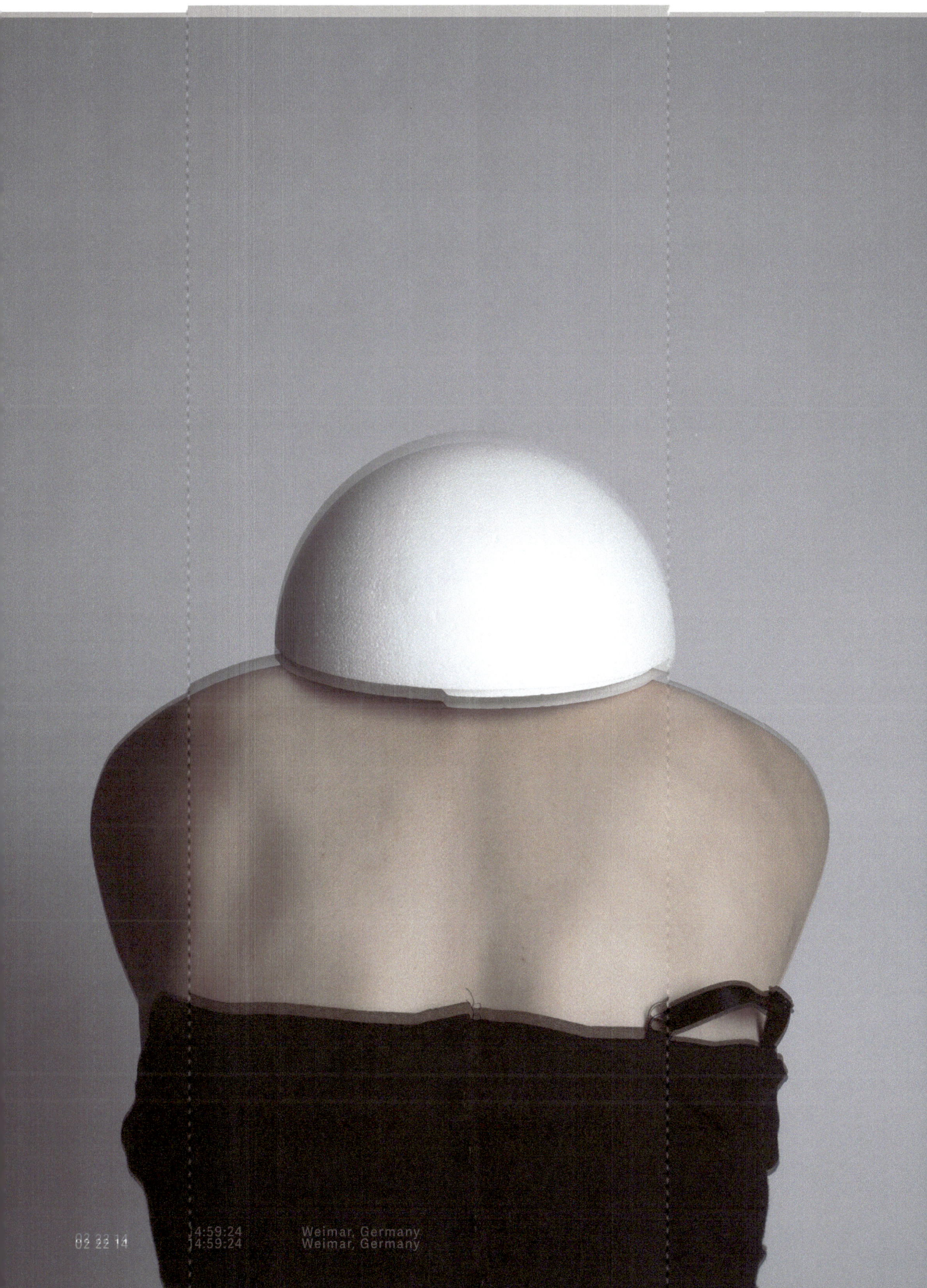

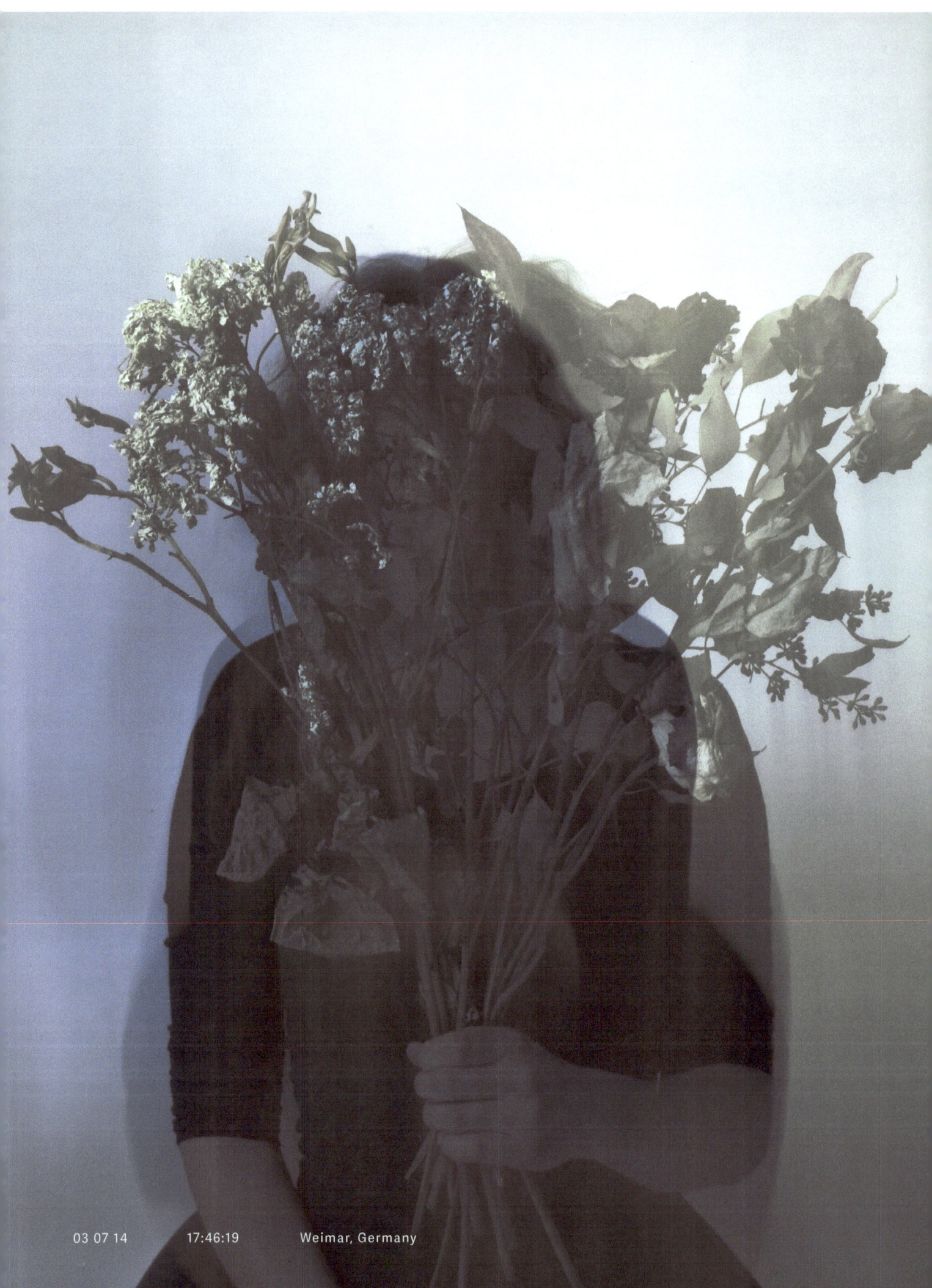

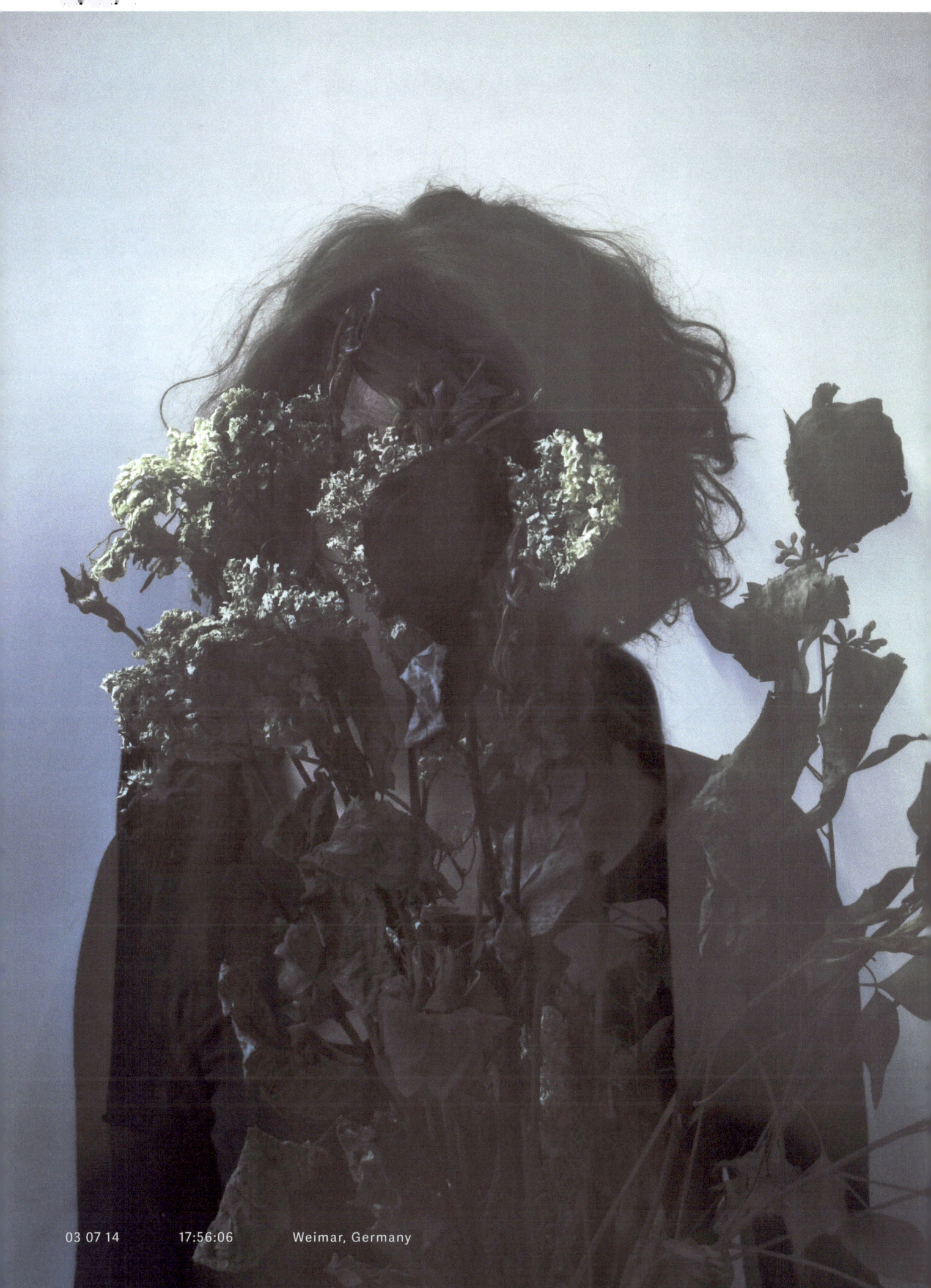

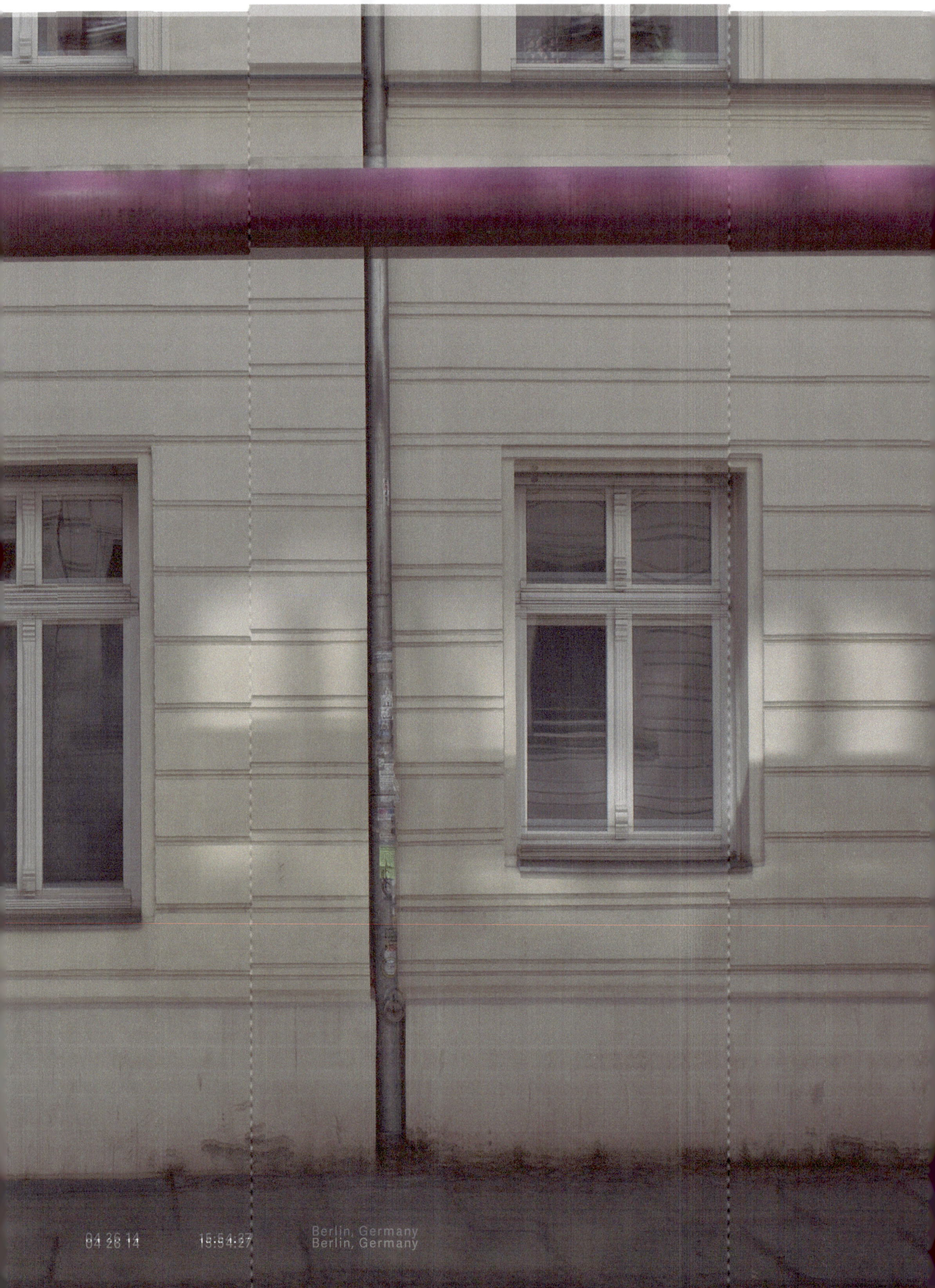

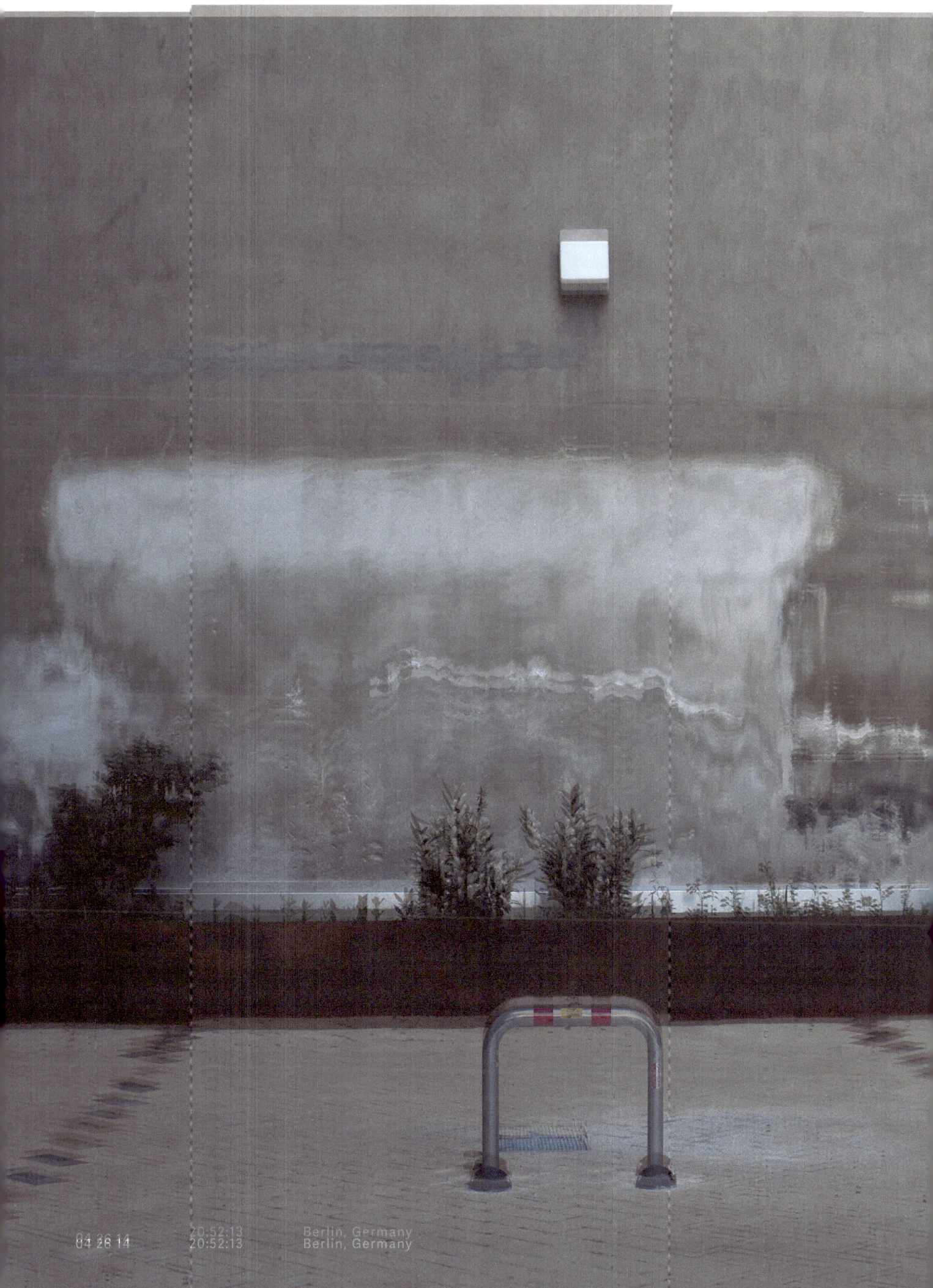

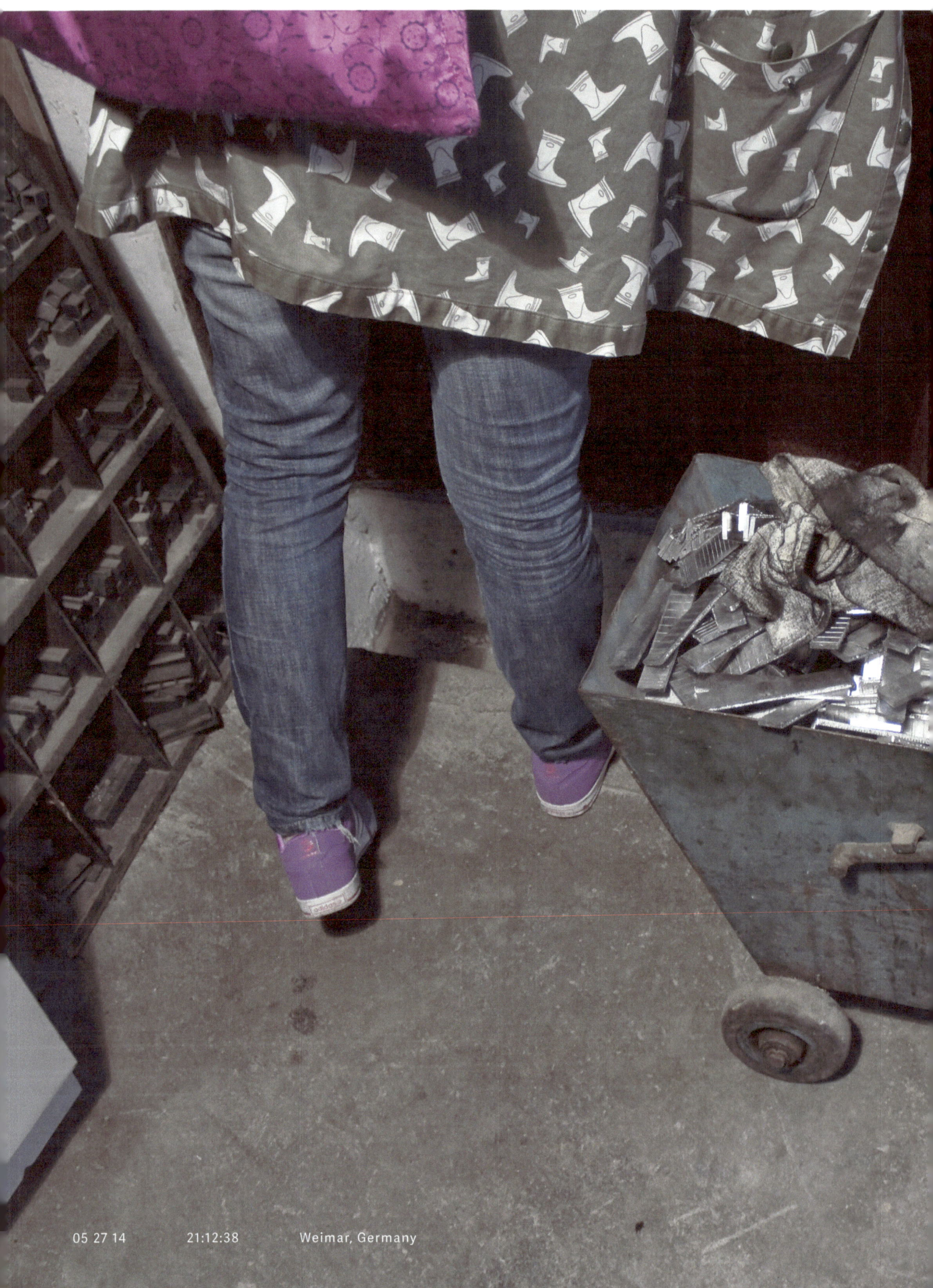

05 27 14   21:12:38   Weimar, Germany

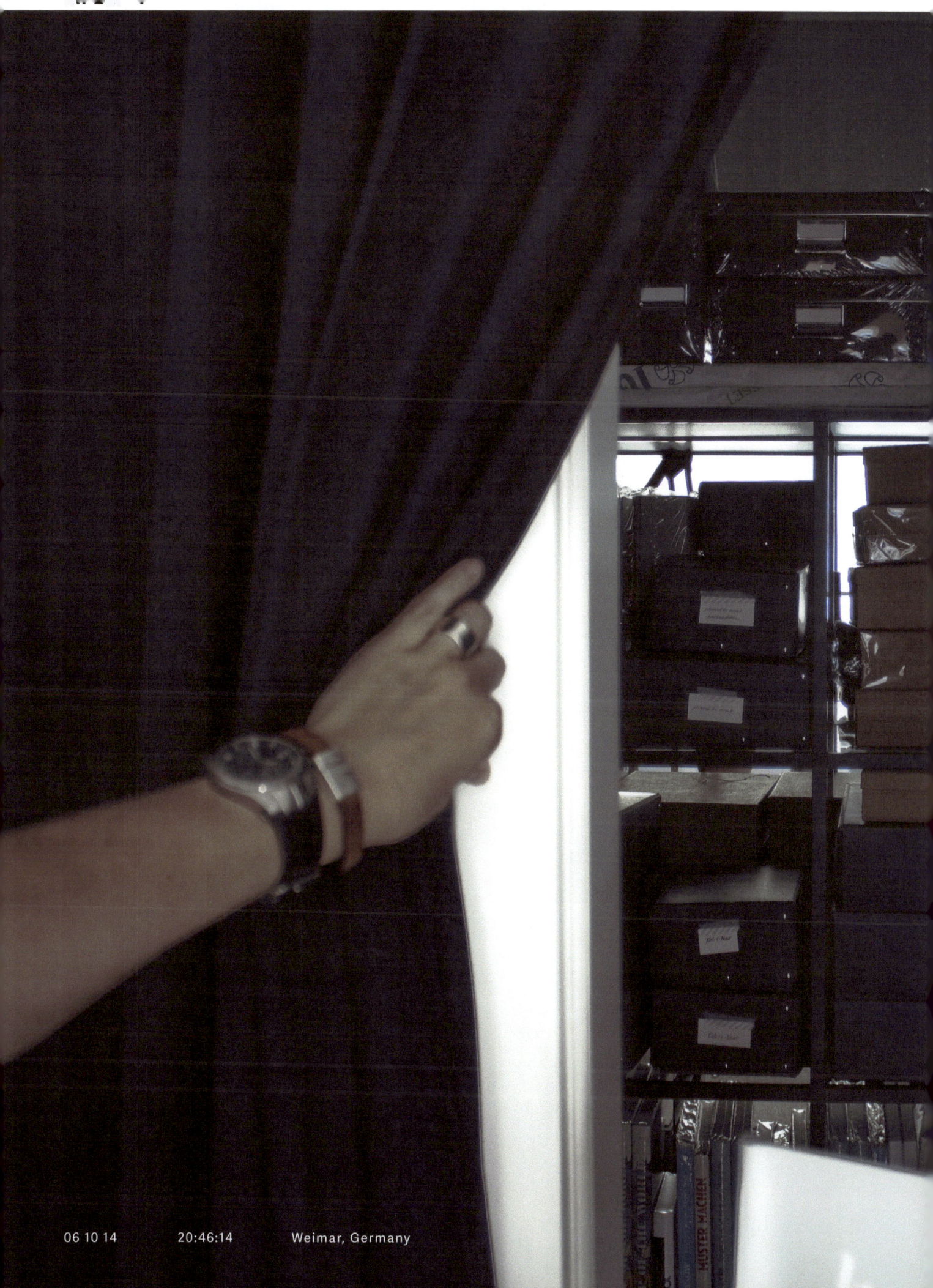

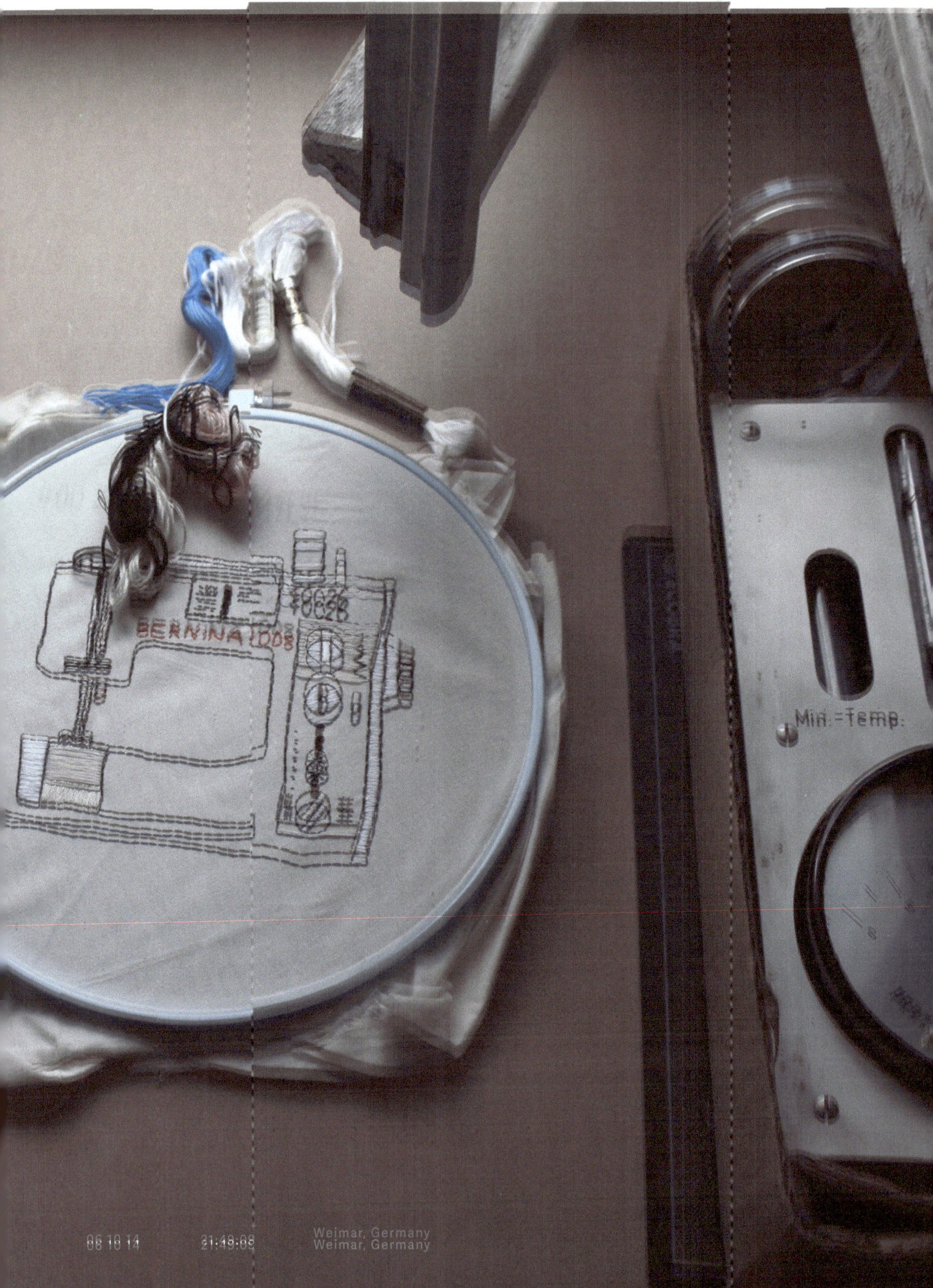

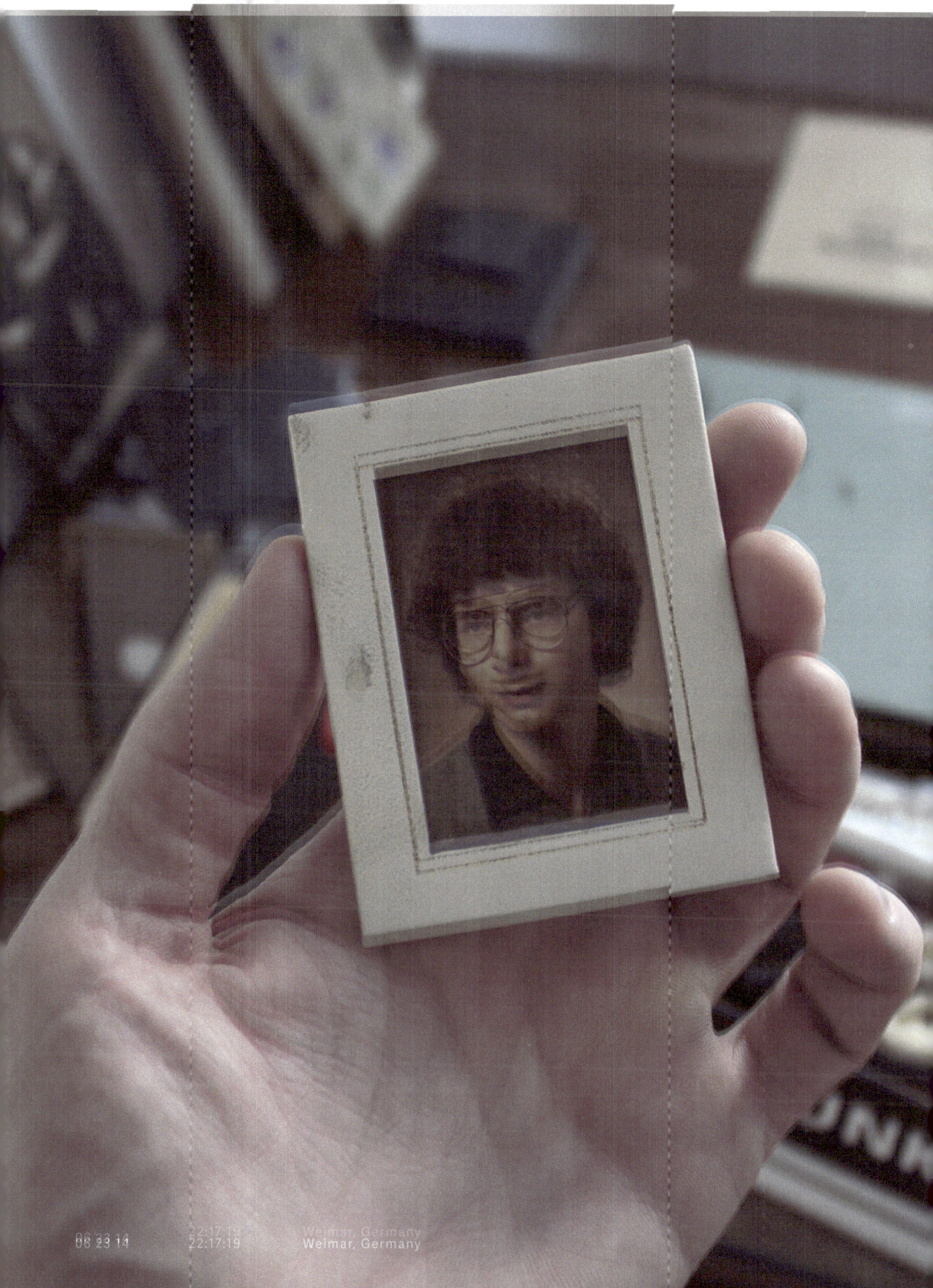

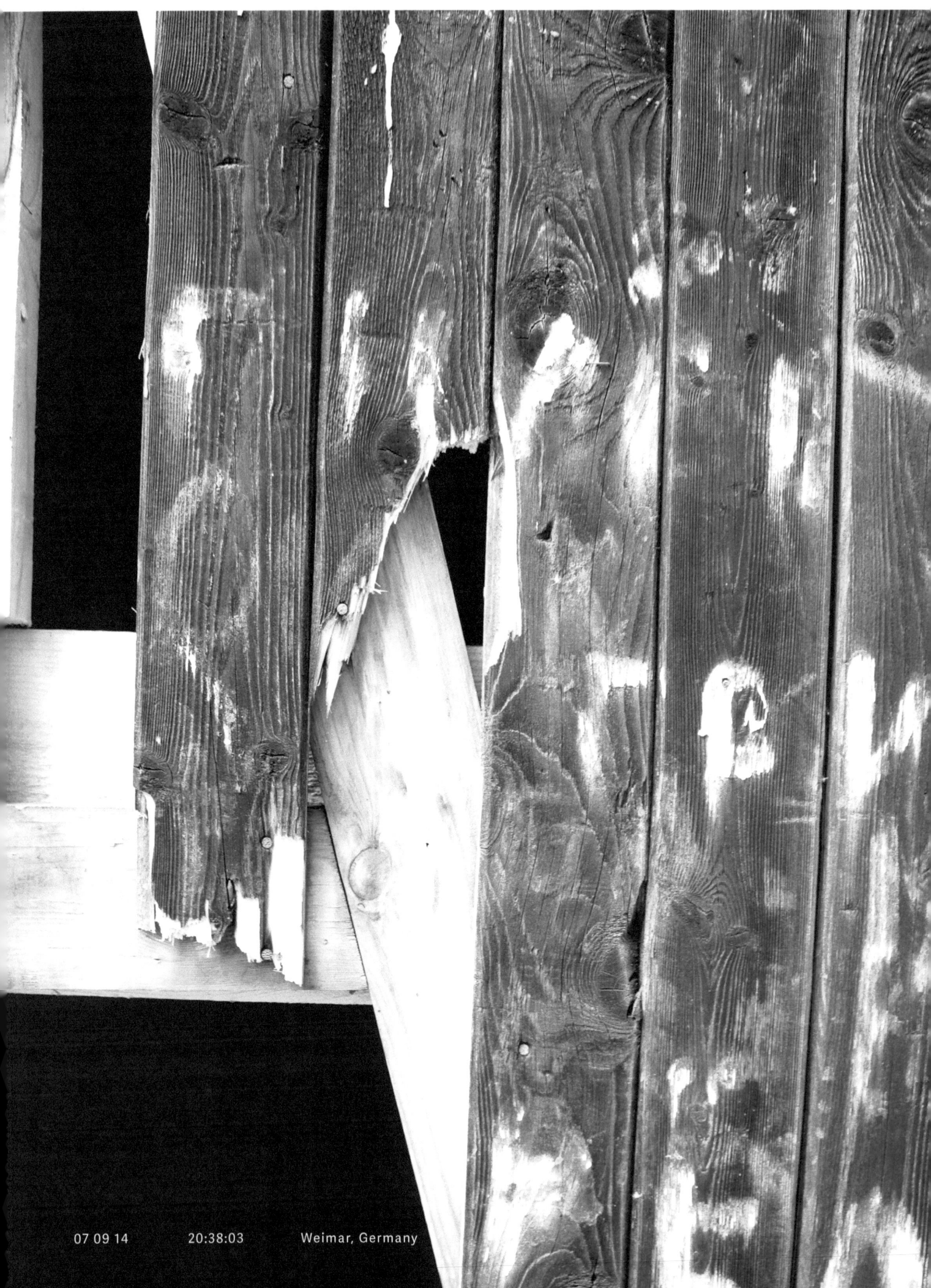
07 09 14   20:38:03   Weimar, Germany

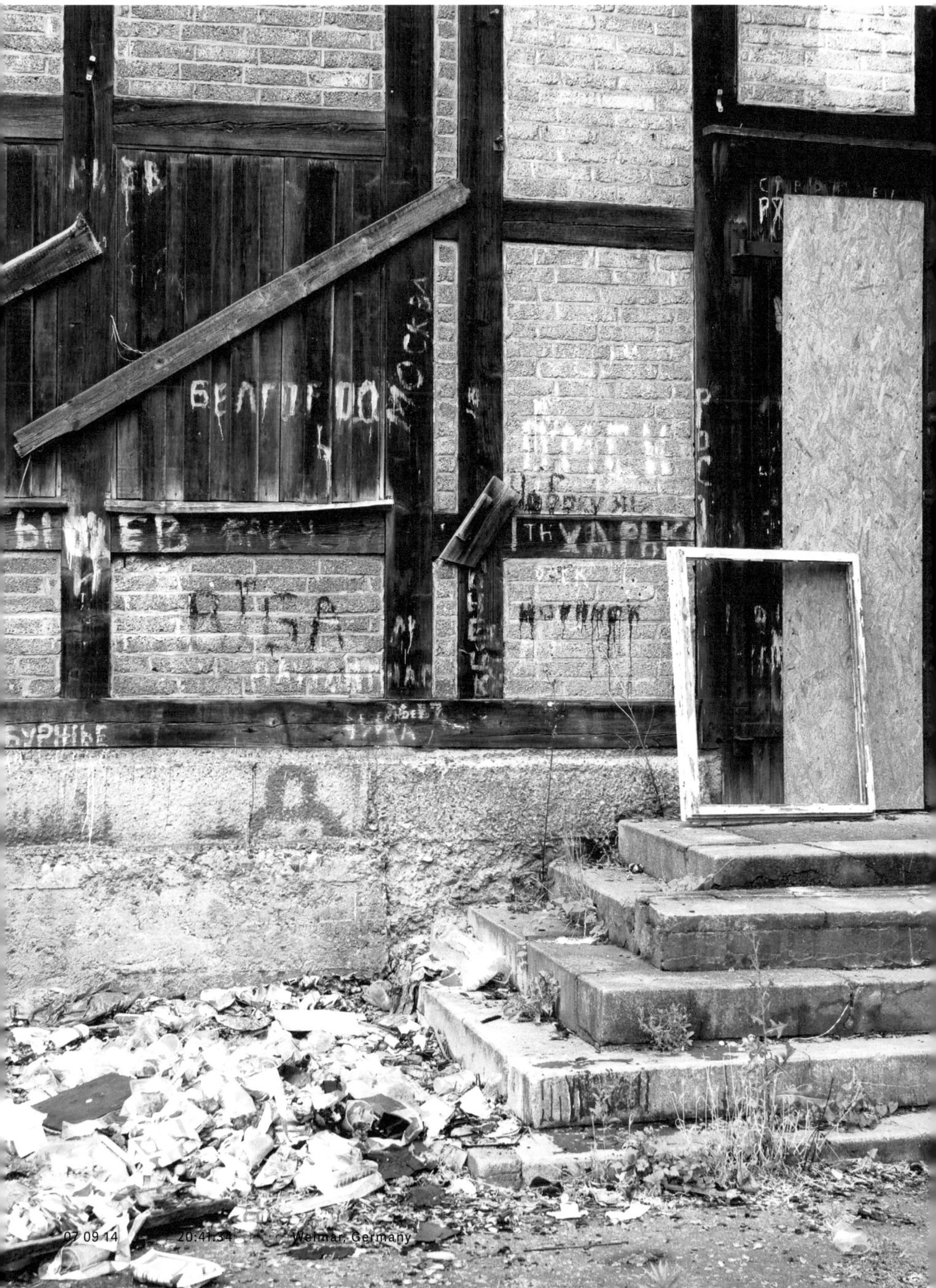

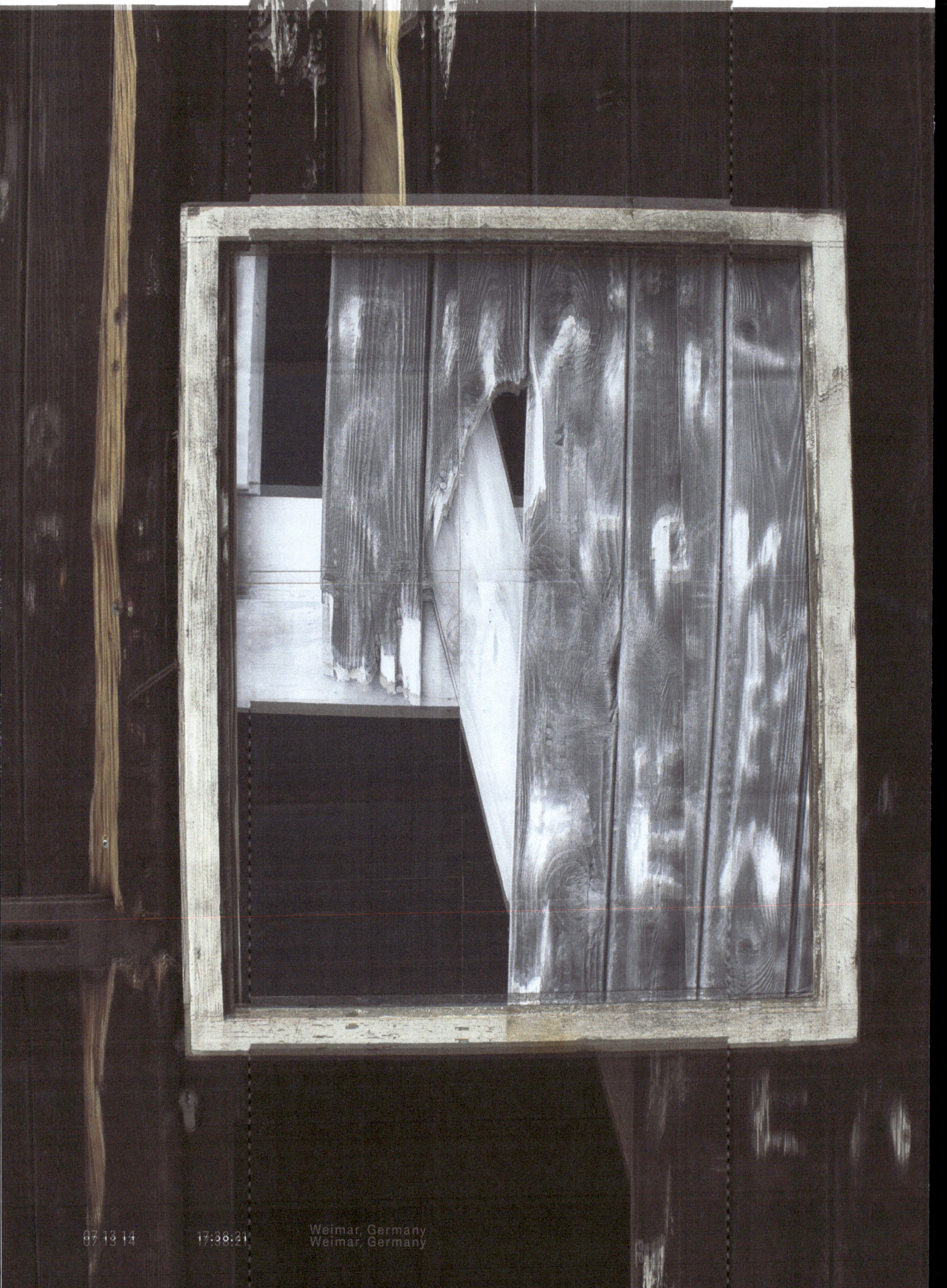

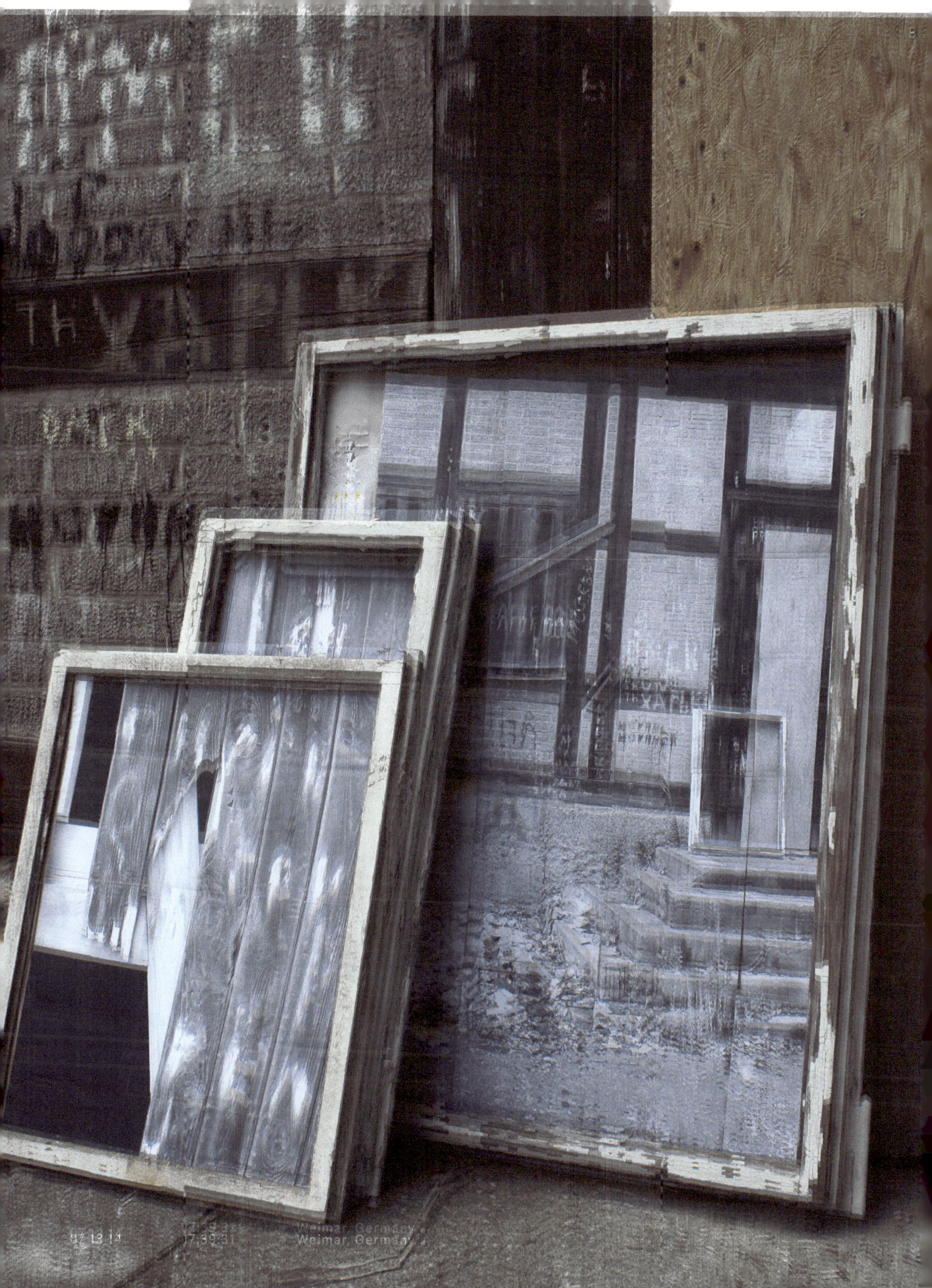

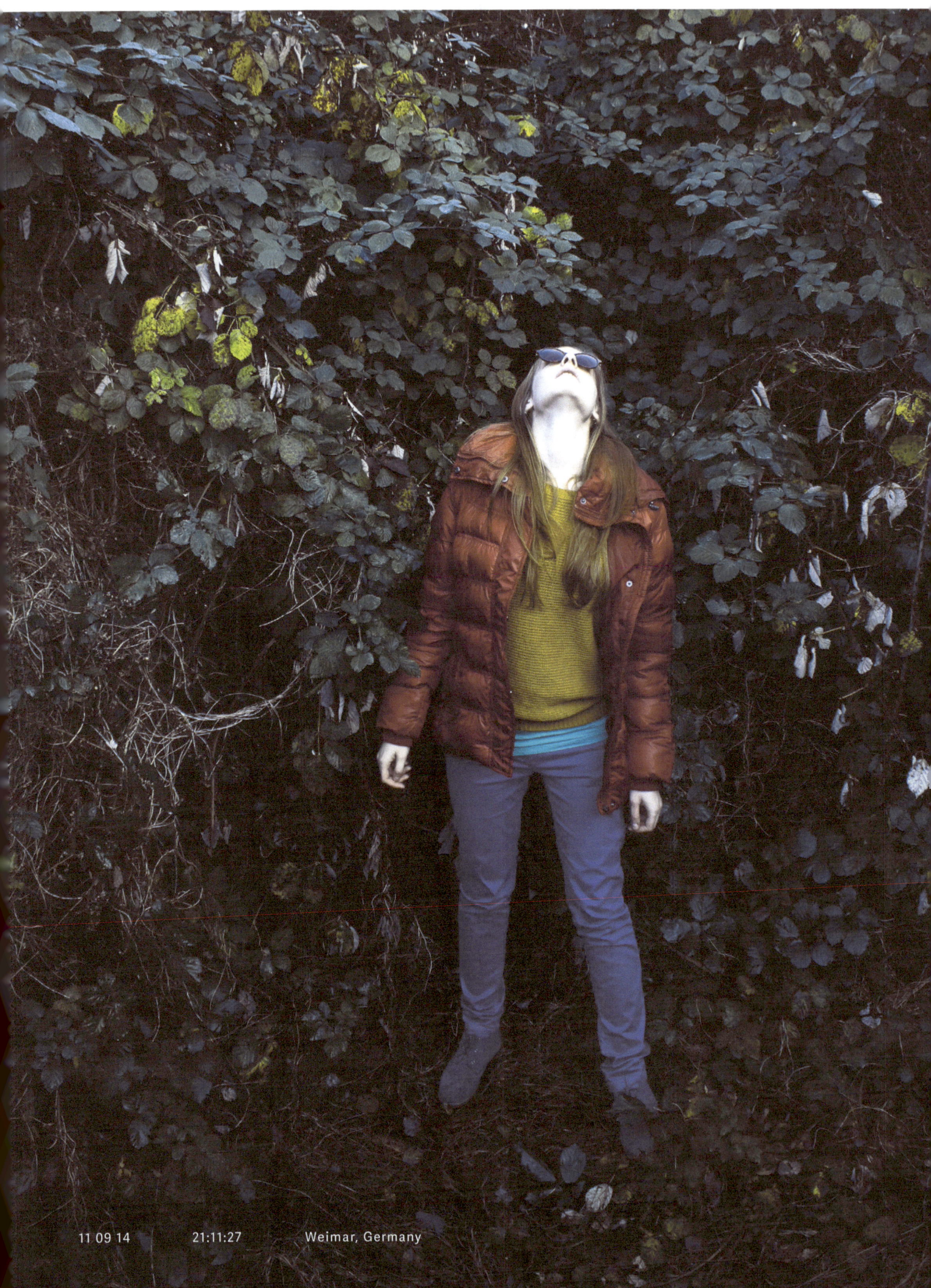

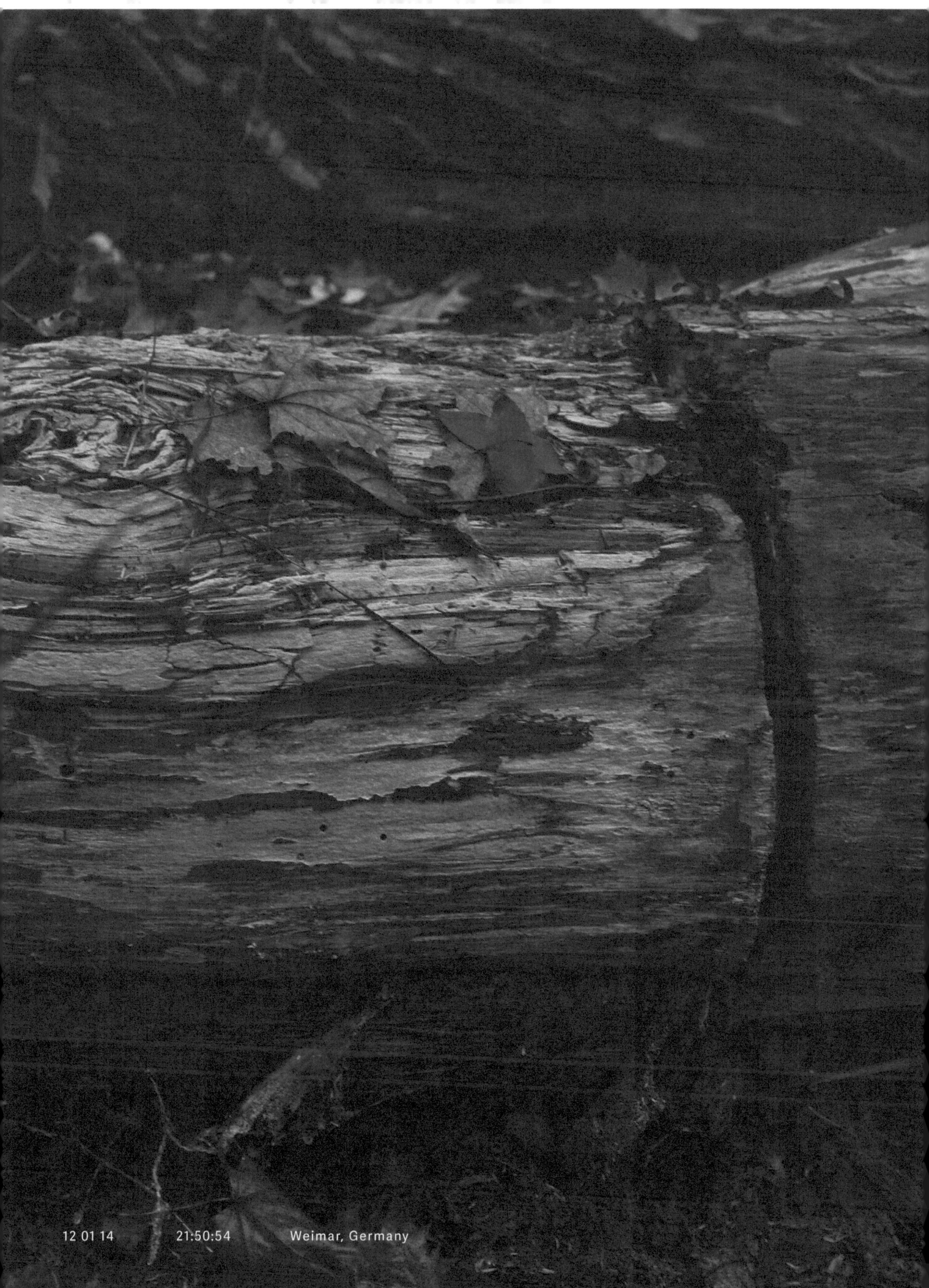

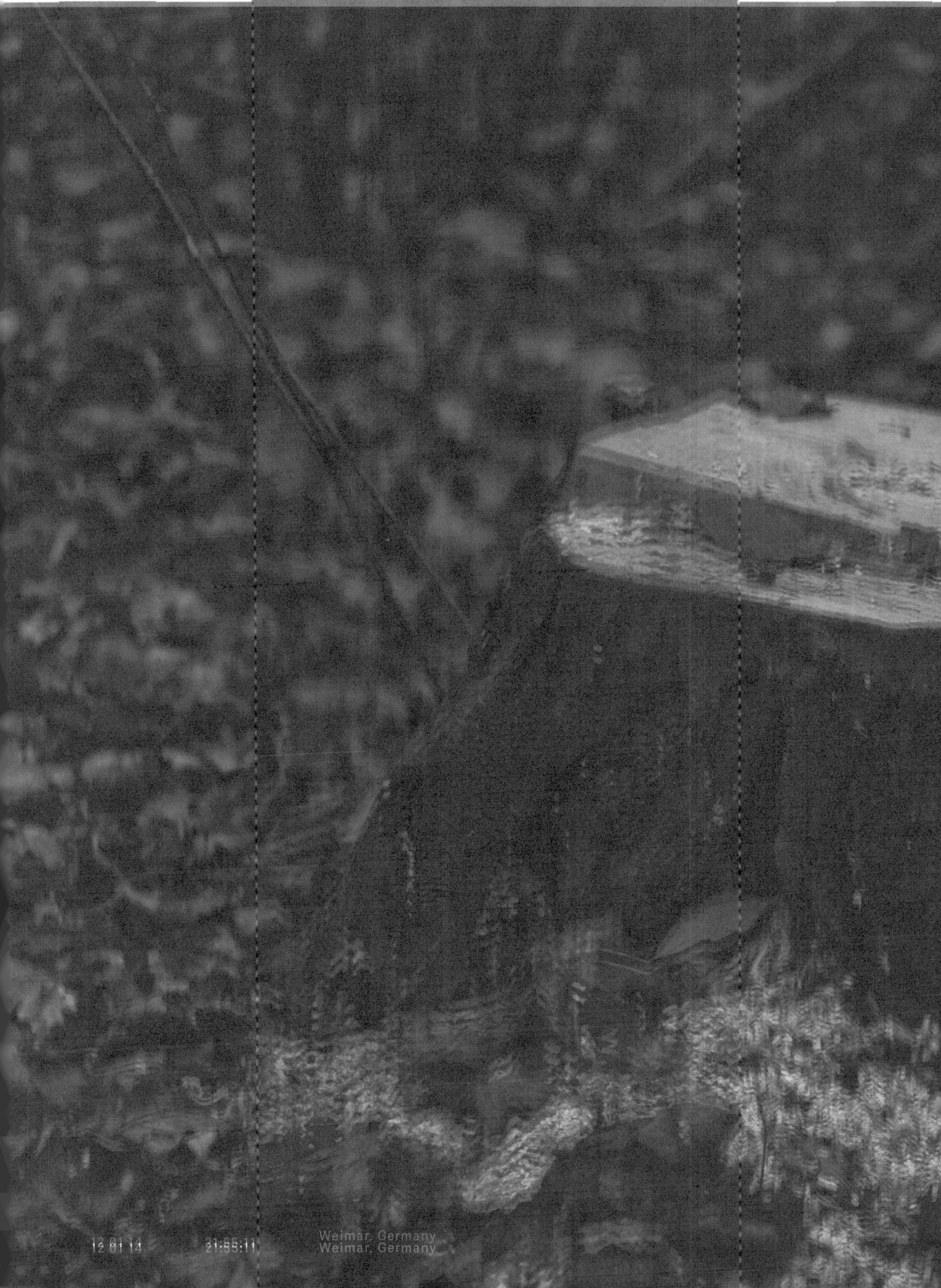

This edition of Escape Artist features photographs by Brian Bixby. All photos were taken in 2014. Photographs appear chronologically and are stamped with the date, time and location.

Models (in order of appearance): Kathrin Leisch, Alexandra Hopp, Lucia Martinez, Christine Hill, Brian Bixby, Becca Sparkes.

ESCAPE ARTIST PUBLISHING
7 8 9 10 14 13 12 11
© escape artist - 2014
photographs 2014 - brian bixby
copyright © 2014 by brian bixby - all rights reserved
photography courtesy of the artist
brianbixby.com
printed in germany